Growing Older
by George Ancona

E. P. Dutton   New York

To Chichi, Oma, and Opa

Library of Congress Cataloging in Publication Data

Ancona, George.   Growing Older.
SUMMARY: Presents anecdotal remembrances of older people
as told to the author.
1. Aged—United States—Biography—Juvenile literature.
[1. Old age—Biography]   I. Title.
HQ1064.U5A648   1978   301.43′5′0922   [920]   78-7605
ISBN: 0-525-31050-9

Published in the United States by E. P. Dutton, a Division
of Sequoia-Elsevier Publishing Company, Inc., New York

Published simultaneously in Canada by Clarke,
Irwin & Company Limited, Toronto and Vancouver

Editor: Ann Troy   Designer: George Ancona
Printed in the U.S.A.   First Edition
10 9 8 7 6 5 4 3 2 1

When my mother and father came to this country, they left their parents behind in Mexico. I knew I had a grandmother because she would write letters to me. Her writing was very beautiful. The pages were filled with lovely curves. She wrote in Spanish, and my mother would read the letters to me. I still have them. When I finished high school, I went to visit her for the first time.

It would have been nice to grow up having my grandparents near.

Perhaps that is why I enjoy visiting with older people and listening to them talk about themselves and the times before I was born. This book is a collection of anecdotes as they were told to me. They were transcribed from the tape recordings I made on my visits. I hope you enjoy them as much as I did.

Ask your grandparents for their stories. If you don't have grandparents nearby, borrow or adopt some, as certain Indian tribes do (see page 18). Then you can have a Granny or a Gramps, or an Oma or Opa, or a Baba or Zayda, or a Nonna or Nonno. Someday you can tell their stories to your grandchildren and add your own story.

On a hot August afternoon, JOE COLE sat on the porch of his log cabin, talking and joking with his friends and family. Mr. Cole is a trader and dealer of antiques. He lives just outside Smithville, Texas. A few miles away from his home is the roadside stand where he sells or trades his wares.

Yep, I'm one man that you're looking at that rode a deer one time. My Grandma had this old deer fenced in. He was about seven years old with a beautiful rack of horns. He would lift his head and lay those horns on his back. He had a little bell on him. I used to play with him all the time.

After lunch my Grandma always set on the porch knitting socks, with my old-maid aunt and bachelor uncle. One day I was out there prowling around the corral. There was a big old log that had salt on it for the cattle to eat. This old deer he come up, licking that salt. This time I reached up and grabbed him by the rack of horns. I pulled, and he pulled me up. As he lifted me, I just eased my leg up over him. When I lay down on that scoundrel, he jumped right over that log with me on him.

I stayed on him. We went down about fifteen or twenty steps when Grandma heard that bell. She looked up and saw me sitting on that deer just as he start running away. Well, Grandma, my aunt and uncle all hopped off the porch, and here they is coming just as hard as they can. Course, Grandma is at the end, she being eighty years old, but she's coming.

I always heard my uncle say that someday that old deer was going back to where he came from. As I rode him across the prairie, I got to thinking, "This old deer is going back now." Well, I decided to get off. I put my head down and let loose. You could step off a freight train going sixty miles an hour and you wouldn't roll as much as I did. I just lay there and played like I was badly hurt. That way, I knew I wouldn't get a whipping.

I remember Uncle Willie had me in his arms as he trotted home. Wasn't anything wrong with me. They carried me back to the porch, bathed my face, and I come to. I mean I had a nasty fall.

They didn't have no doctors in them days. If

Joe Cole as a baby

you got knocked out, they pour water over you, blowed in your mouth, and if you didn't come to, the next day they buried you. For snakebites and spider bites they would put a drop of kerosene into a spoonful of sugar and you swallowed that. Sugar and kerosene oil were used for sore throats, bad colds, and stopped-up chests.

We lived on a farm and ranch together. When you got big enough, you went to work. My daddy had lots of cattle, and the farm raised cotton. School never did start till the fifteenth of September, and it was out the first of May. They needed the kids . . . picking cotton, chopping cotton. When I was thirteen years old, I could plow, yoke steers, work oxen.

I'm seventy-seven years old, and I never went but one day to school. That ain't no lie. We lived eight miles from school, and I had to walk. Well, the first day of school they got me up kind of late. They got me off in such a hurry, darn if I didn't forget my lunch. When I got to school, the kids were just turning out for lunch. So I turned around and walked back home and got it.

By the time I got back to school, they was turning out to go home. Eight and eight is sixteen, sixteen and sixteen is thirty-two miles I'd walked that day. The next day I felt so drowsy I just never went back to school. One day is all I went. If I hadn't forgot my lunch, I'd be President of the United States.

I'm pretty smart like it is. I guess it's a good thing I didn't get no education, 'cause everybody thinks I'm a darn rascal anyway.

Sign leading to Joe Cole's cabin

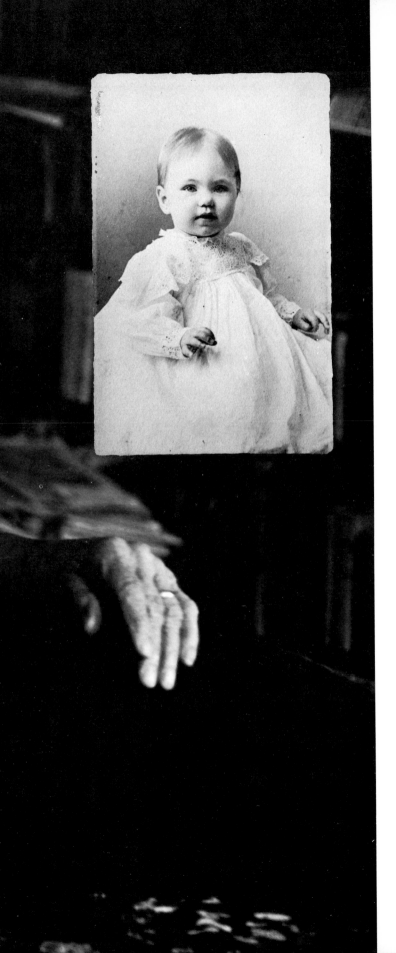

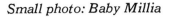

A long driveway leads to **MILLIA DAVENPORT***'s house, where she lives alone. Beds of flowers surround the house, and there is also a vegetable garden where she spends her time when she isn't traveling. Inside, the walls are covered with books and pictures. She enjoys the company of good friends, good food, and good conversation.*

When I was a little girl, I used to run away from home all the time. I had a cousin who played football at school, and I would try to get into the game to see him. My parents tied me to a long line as though I were a little dog. I must have been three. An awful snoop.

One day I was sitting in my high chair at lunch. My father, mother, and aunt had books and papers propped up in front of them. They were reading while they ate. Our maid, Mary Cox, said, "Won't it be nice for the baby when she learns to read?" I thought this was a dandy idea. Mary taught me C-A-T and D-O-G. I'm told I was able to read by the time I was two and a half. I've been reading ever since. It was a black woman who taught me to read. All those professors (my parents and aunt), it never would have occurred to them to do anything about it.

Making "mud pies," a half sandwich on round pumpernickel bread

We lived right on Cold Spring Harbor. I had a little motorboat. When I didn't want to take a piano lesson, I'd get out in the middle of the harbor and my motor would break down. Everybody could see that little Millia was in no real trouble. She could always row back. I didn't have to come home if I didn't feel like it.

My father didn't believe in knives for little girls. Around my neck on a shoestring (he did believe in shoestrings) hung a very good steel shoehorn. With that I could open clams, mussels, and oysters. I would eat my way through the day without having to come home.

When I was fourteen, my mother became pregnant, and I was sent to Paris, where my aunt lived. She settled me in a riotous summer place belonging to an order of nuns who didn't have to wear habits. They dressed like everybody else. I stayed both in their country place and in their Paris place.

A marvelous thing happened when I was in their country place. It was in the Bois de Chaville. I had a donkey cart which I drove around through the woods. There was a large open space

in which the Count de Lambert had an airplane, a biplane. It looked as if it was made of paper and string. I used to sit there and look at it.

One day the count, dressed in a long white coat and goggles, asked me if I wouldn't like to have a ride in the plane. I said yes. I tied up my donkey and off we went. One turn around over the woods and back. That was really lovely.

In Paris the only bathroom they had belonged to the head of the school. She never used it. We had to bathe in a bowl. First we would put a sheet over us, then take our clothes off. Then we would slop water on ourselves, dry ourselves, and get dressed . . . all under the sheet. Well, I didn't care much for this. I thought I should be allowed to go to the student hostel and bathe. The nuns didn't want to have to put on their hats, gloves, and veils to take me, so I was allowed to go all by myself.

I had a marvelous year in Paris with my aunt. The old girl really knew Paris inside and out. It was my first time away from home. When I got back to America, I had a very nice six-month-old little brother.

My mother was a great gardener. She drove me absolutely nuts because she always needed my help. I thought I would never remember anything she told me. I would close my eyes and ears. My mother was always telling me, "Weed as you go, and always go a different way." This is the most sensible thing anybody has ever said to me. I've told every kid that has ever gardened with me, "Weed as you go, and always go a different way."

My mother was also a very beautiful seamstress. She made me lovely clothes, but she wouldn't teach me to sew. She thought I was such a lazy good-for-nothing child. In school in France I was a very good mender. I mended all the vestments for the priests. The nuns taught me to make lace.

My father was a scientist, and I made charts for him. I also had to work in the library. They decided little Millia was very bright and didn't take any time to do her homework. So I was enslaved at the age of twelve to a scientific library.

I've had an awful lot of various experiences, all of which came in very handy in my work as a theatrical designer. I'm the last of the old guard who could make a costume from scratch: design it, make it, cut, fit, do everything.

When I retired, I started to work on a costume book. I worked for ten solid years on that book. In fact, I've had a good time doing it, and it turned out to be the classic work of my life.

I've had a really lovely life. I've been almost everywhere in the world. Now I'm going to Europe and then to Egypt. That will take me back to London for a day, where I'll buy my seeds. When I come back, I'll have time to plant the peas. If the peas aren't in the ground by the fifteenth of March, you won't have any peas. I always have a terribly good time wherever I go. I make lots of friends of all ages and shapes.

I'm in my eighty-third year. My plans are to live as long as I can and have as good a time as I can. I used to work sixteen hours a day. Now if I work six, I know I'm ready to lie down and read. If my eyes aren't working right, I sleep. When I wake up, if my eyes are fine, I just read all night. I live my life the way it comes, according to what I've got.

CHARLIE DARTER *left his hometown in Texas to join the army during World War II. He returned to marry and settle down to farm. A hunting accident injured his leg and kept him from farming. He went to work in the post office, and later retired. He now raises a few head of cattle. Together with his wife, Louise, he grows the fruits and vegetables they preserve for the winter.*

*O*ne of my earliest recollections is when my daddy took me down to the river one day. He was going to gather pecans. He set me up in the trunk of a tree, and he says, "Now, son, I want you to look across the river. I want you to be real quiet, and if you see a deer, just whistle softly. I'll get my rifle and get us a deer."

So I sat there no telling how long. Pretty soon I see this buck deer coming down the other side of the river. I could see it had horns. I give a low whistle. Daddy puts down his pecan-gathering sack and takes up his thirty-thirty. We see the deer jump in the river and start swimming toward us. When he comes up on the bank, Daddy shoots it. We dressed it and had it to eat.

That's when we lived down in the log cabin. My mother taught us. I'd never been to school, church, or anything. For church we'd meet in what we call a brush arbor. They put up some poles and some cedar shakes to make shade, and they'd preach. There was no school. We were thirty-two miles from anywhere.

It was all right for fishing and hunting and raising cattle, but the place wasn't any good for sending kids to school. So we moved to Round Rock, where they put me in the second grade. I was eight.

There were many rattlesnakes around there, and you had to watch all the time. One day when I was at the age where I liked to make roads in the yard, I made myself a wagon out of a tobacco box. So there I was in the yard pulling my wagon and having the best old time. I went to park that little wagon in the shade. Well, there in that shade was a rattlesnake. I eased that hand back and went to the house.

My daddy was washing up, and he called, "Son, hand me the towel over there." "Dad, I'll make a trade with you. I'll hand you the towel, and you come kill a rattlesnake." He said, "I'll trade that way." Well, there were so many rattlesnakes that he always kept a weeding hoe by the back door. He killed it. I'd rather shoot them, but a weeding hoe helps to equalize things.

EMMA ANCONA *is called Chichi by her grandchildren and friends, just as she called her grandmother in Yucatán, Mexico. She is a widow, living alone in the same house she shared with her husband. Her greatest pleasure is to have the house filled with family and friends, for whom she will prepare huge Mexican meals. In addition to her involvement with family, neighbors, and friends, she belongs to the local senior citizens' group.*

My name is Emma Graziana Díaz Triay de Ancona. I was born in 1903 in Espita, a small town in Yucatán, Mexico. My mother had ten children, and I was the spoiled brat of the family, the pet of my father. When I was small, my father would visit his mother in Mérida, the big city. I used to jump on the train and go with him. I used to get new clothes and everything.

One time when I was eight years old, I wanted a doll. My father went to Mérida and bought me one. I was the only girl in the whole town with a doll. I convinced my mother and father that I wanted to baptize the doll and have a party. So we invited some children. Everybody thinks my mother and father crazy.

I baptized the doll. They made a nice dress for the doll. One of the boys dressed as a priest, another a godfather, and a girl was the godmother. We had a piñata, and we had ice cream. We had cards with the name of the doll. It's one thing in my life I never forget. The party lasted for about four or five hours. The whole town was there, about thirty, forty children. We had tamales, tacos, ice cream. The ice cream was made by hand. We would turn the handle for hours and hours. All the kids took turns.

For piñatas we used clay pots. Inside the pots they put candy with two white pigeons, *palomas.* Then they take the piñata and they pull it up and down, while we try to break it with a stick. When we broke the piñata, the *palomas* flew away in the air. That was something very beautiful, very beautiful. Now they make piñatas out of paper and cardboard because some children would get hurt with the broken clay pots.

We used to have piñatas on horseback. Instead of a piñata, we hung a watermelon from a rope, and they pulled it up and down. I used to ride

Mrs. Ancona as a baby with her father and brothers

With granddaughter in nursery school

a horse and hit the watermelon. I was the only girl who'd do it. Once the horse threw me down, but I didn't give up. I went back again.

We used to have dances. When my father was living, I was little and he would take me. I would sit there and watch. When I was eighteen my brother would take me and all the neighbors. The day of the dance they stretched a wire from two trees in the center of town. Hanging from it were colored ribbons with a ring at the bottom. Each ribbon had the name of a girl on it. The boys would race their horses and try to catch a ring with a stick. The girl whose name was on the ribbon was the boy's dance partner for the evening. If somebody else wanted to dance with her, they had to ask his permission. We used to dance waltzes, polkas, tangos, pasos dobles, and jaranas.

When it's time to stop dancing, everybody goes to the buffet tables. In those days we had refreshments made of pure fruit. We don't know what is soda. The boys sit with you and the family. When somebody say it is eleven or twelve o'clock, my father would say, "Why stop? In this world there is much misery and little happiness. So when you're happy, stop the clock and continue." I always remember that. When I'm happy in one place, I never worry to see the time. I let the time go by. That's why I always say to anybody who says, "Oh, it's late!" I say, "When you're happy, try to live this life because you never know about tomorrow."

We had a servant called Tomasa. She was Indian. The Indians know a secret so their hair never turns white. You see an Indian always has black hair. I remember this woman so well because she used to wash my hair all the time. There's a fruit in Yucatán that grows on a cactus vine called pitahaya. It's a little fruit with small black seeds. Every time she wash my hair she takes a piece of that vine and she put it in the water. She squeezed, and it was like glue. She would rinse my hair with that. She would tell me I never going to get white hair. I'm seventy-three, and I have very little white hair. All my family have white hair, even my own son.

GEORGE WILLIAM HARRIS *was watching an Indian dance contest with one of his grandsons. The dancers were young men from around Oklahoma City. Friends and families formed a large ring around the dancers. In the center sat the drummers and the older people who sang. Mr. Harris is a retired truck driver. He takes care of his wife, who is not well. At home he does the cooking and cleaning.*

I'm a Sauk and Fox Indian. I was born in 1912 and grew up with five brothers and a sister. We farmed eight acres. We raised cotton, corn, horses, and hogs. When I was a boy, we played with a rag ball and blackjack sticks. Sometimes girls played with us. We'd swim and ride horses. When we grew up, we had guns to go hunting. Little boys would go hunting with their fathers or go alone. An Indian can't get lost. He knows the stars.

I grew up in the woods. We built our houses of wood and the bark of elm trees. We make the frames out of the wood poles and tied the bark on them like shingles. In summertime we stayed in this bark house. In the middle we cooked. The smoke goes out the roof.

Then we make a cattail house we call a winter house. Them cattails grow in water. We cut them off and weave them together and tie them on top the frame. The water sheds off them. It was warm in there.

I went to school in a one-room little building. Went up to the eighth grade all in one room. We all walked. No school buses then. We'd get up, snow waist-deep sometimes, and go to school. I went from there to a government school. Stayed three months and didn't like it, so I come home and went to work.

Three children who lost their fathers adopted me in our ceremonial ways. In our tribe if somebody loses their dad or mother, they'll get somebody else to take their place. The oldest boy in the family comes with tobacco and says, "We want you to be our Dad." If you take the tobacco, they'll call you to their place and feed you.

Before they feed you, they take everything off, clean you up, and put on new clothes. They paint your cheeks and around your eyes with red or blue and white. They have new dishes filled with food. You eat. Then they wash the dishes and bundle them up. Them's yours.

From then on you look after them children. When you see one they say, "Hello Dad." Or you say, "Hello Son" or "Daughter" or "Nephew" or "Brother." That's the way we do from way back. I adopted five brothers, and I got an adopted mother still living. When I go over there, she says, "Hello Sonny, sit down and eat." There's no literature for this. It's all in the mind passed on to this time.

ANN SHADLOW *lives in a suburb of Oklahoma City with her husband and grandchildren. Her Indian name is Pretty Wing. While she talked about her life, her teen-age grandchildren were in their room listening to recordings of Indian music and stringing beads for their costumes. The whole family was preparing for a festival that evening.*

I was raised by my grandparents. They had full control of us. We were raised real gentle. No harsh words. They would set us down and talk to us.

My grandfather was French and Indian. His father was a French trader, and his mother a Cheyenne woman. My grandmother was English and Indian. She didn't speak English.

My father was a tall, stalwart, and handsome man. A jim-dandy. My mother died, and he never remarried. He was real helpful to me and my children. He liked to cook and run my house. I just loved my father. He was a good man. I kept him when he became old and till he died.

I never knew my mother. All I remember about my mother was sadness because she was ill. She was about forty when she died, and then we went to boarding school. I was ten. I hadn't gone to school till then, but my grandfather tutored me. I had no formal education, but I had a lot of love from my people.

When I was a child, we lived in a big log house. My father built it on my mother's land in the Pine Ridge Reservation. It was Oglala Sioux country. Rolling prairie. It was divided into four rooms. The kitchen had a big wood-burning stove. My father would order things by the big sacks and put them in the cellar. We had flour, sugar, coffee, molasses, and things from the garden. In the middle of the cellar we dug a big hole and put in a pipe filled with hay. We stored our vegetables there for the winter months. It was very cold, and stores were far away. We had a lean-to that led to a big root cellar. Outside, we had a smokehouse. We made our own salt meat, bacon, and ham in the smokehouse. We lived better than folks nowadays.

We were taught and raised that older people came first. I think that my life is richer because I lived close to my grandparents. The aunts and cousins were all very good. I stayed around the old people and enjoyed them. My grandmother lived over the hill in her little log house. Grandmother's house had a dirt roof and floor. They destroyed the house when she died. My grandmother dressed me from the time I was little. We always dressed in our Indian clothes. I wore the long cotton skirts with dark prints and the little high boots. She always tied bells on them so she'd know we were around.

Grandmother and granddaughter in costume

and without costume

Of course we had cattle and horses, and we rode. That was our entertainment. Everyone rode. My mother was a good horsewoman. I rode bareback with my skirt and long hair . . . tomboy. I also rode pigs and calves with my long skirt. There were little streams and arroyos. Nobody said "You might get hurt." My brother and I herded cattle every day. We're a year apart. We'd race and play shinny. It's an old Indian game, a little like hockey. We made our sticks and ball. We'd pick two sides, and the whole family would play.

I only went to school five years. I was fifteen years old when I finished ninth grade, and I had one year of nurses' training. When I first got to boarding school, they asked me if I had ever gone to school. "No," I answered, "I never did go to school." I didn't realize that my grandfather had tutored me. I would read the newspaper to him. He taught me everything in math. I was way up there in math. My half-breed Grandfather Guerrier was the one that taught me to read and write.

At home all I ever heard was Indian. In boarding school we were punished for speaking Indian. We are losing our Indian languages.

There was an essay contest at the boarding school. I wrote about the health among my people. I wanted to grow up and help them with their health problems. I won it, but they tried to take it away from me because I was too young. I was only fourteen years old. Well, I won that one year of nurses' training anyway. The only place I couldn't go into was the obstetrics room, where the babies are born. They said I was too young, but I had already been a midwife twice back home. When I was twelve, I went home where my sister had her babies. She had one in July and one the next year in August. I took care of her till she was on her feet.

When I was sixteen, I married. My husband was Arapaho. My father was very upset because I had married an Indian. Later I discovered why. My father was a half-breed. He didn't belong to this side and he didn't belong to that side. I made up my mind I was not going to be that way. I wanted to be an Indian. When I grew up, I went back to my people, the Cheyenne.

Around here I'm proud and friendly. I'm everybody's Grandma, and that's the way I like to be called. I'm Grandma to men who are pretty near fifty years old.

Every weekday morning RICHARD MAY *leaves his apartment in midtown New York and takes a taxi to work. He works for a company whose offices overlook New York harbor. His job is to enter the daily expenses into a large book and add them up. He doesn't use an adding machine or calculator. At 3 P.M. he leaves his office, cane in hand, and takes a taxi home. The drive takes him past the Brooklyn Bridge, which was opened the year he was born, 1883.*

I was born in Germany. My poor mother had a lot of troubles. She had five children. My father went away with a dancing lady to Berlin and left my mother with the five children. It was not very pleasant. I always took care of her. I can't remember much of my childhood. My mother wasn't able to put me in the gymnasium, which is what they called high school in Germany. It was very expensive. I left school to take a job.

I wanted to learn the English language, so I made up my mind to make a trip to America. I had an uncle and two aunts there. I promised my mother I would return. I arrived in New York in 1902, and I've lived here ever since. I made a trip to California in 1906. I recollect it took me a whole week to get to San Francisco from New York by train. The train had to cross a river at Yuma, Arizona, and there was something wrong with the bridge. We had to stay there overnight. It was so beautiful that night, you thought you could touch the stars. It was something I never experienced before.

Six years after I came to America, I went back to visit my mother for the first time. I stayed there for six weeks, and I couldn't stand it anymore. I had to go back to America. That's my place. I loved the Americans. Everything was free here.

I met my wife here on the boardwalk in Rockaway. I fell in love with her right away. She was a beautiful girl. I was twenty-six. She liked me, and we called on each other. We became engaged and married. In 1963 my poor wife passed away, and ever since then I have lived here alone.

Old is a matter of the mind. I feel young at ninety-five. I still have youthful ideas. I don't want to be old. I personally adapt to the changes of living. I can't compare the modern way of living to the one I came from. According to my own ideas, it's not for the better. The young may be happy with it, but it isn't the solid life we used to have, the family life of former years. Children leave their homes because they can't get along with their parents. They have different ideas. I left home to learn another language. But I never forgot my mother's ideas. I'm an old-fashioned man, which I want to be. The young people do not accept my ideas.

PAULINE BRODY *lives alone in the house where she raised her family. She enjoys going for walks in the countryside. Once a week she visits her sister in New York City, where she can see people from all over the world. She also travels frequently to visit her children and grandchildren who live in different parts of the country.*

We lived in a small town in Lithuania. My father was a rabbi. He taught the children who would come to his school early in the morning carrying lanterns. There they would stay until the end of the day.

When he came home, we children were not supposed to make any noise. We had dinner together and if we laughed that was no good. My mother was very tolerant, but my father we were afraid of.

My father was a reader. There were books in the house all the time. I used to read Russian stories and Grimm's fairy tales. One of my favorites was about Hansel and Gretel and the horrible witch they threw in the fire. Then I would tell it to my brothers and sisters, and they would shiver and we would have such a good time.

Pauline, after she came to America

My mother thought I should learn something in dressmaking, so I was sent to work for a dressmaker. She would teach me, but I never learned. The only thing I learned was beautiful Jewish songs. We would sit down to sew and sing. All I could do was pull out the basting.

In the evening people walked back and forth on the main street. That was the street where everybody goes "spazieren." That's the German and Jewish word which means taking a walk. When I was fourteen the young men would pass and tip their hats. We would count how many tips we got. That was the big excitement of the evening. Everybody walked: the doctors, the lawyers, everybody.

When I was fifteen I came to America. I came alone to go to school. I stayed on Ellis Island in New York harbor for a week. Everything was so new to me. Especially the toilets. We didn't know that we had to pull a chain to flush.

I worked in a garment factory on an electric sewing machine. The machines were going so

Off for a walk and a visit to a neighbor

fast it was terrible. They sat me with five hundred other people on a belt system. The noise was terrific. I still remember the noise of that horrible thing.

I was staying with an aunt and uncle who lived on the top floor of an apartment building. When I came home after work, there was nothing to do. I remember my aunt would cook the same thing every single day. She cooked barley soup with a piece of meat in it. Ugh. I couldn't look at barley soup for a long time.

Then I met some girls from Europe and we got an apartment together. We started to live very nicely. I was about sixteen years old. It was easy to move. We had nothing.

We used to go to night school. Nearby was a place where boys would come and they'd fight. I never saw a fight before in my life. They were boxing and I thought they were killing each other. I tried to stop them. I didn't know a word of English and I didn't know what I was doing. One man pulled me away and started to tell me

that this was a sport, not a fight. I couldn't understand for two men to hit each other. "You'll get hurt!" I would shout. My life is one of not accepting. When there were strikes in the needle trades, I was on the picket line.

Getting older is not a bad thing. You change a lot. Many things become unimportant. Such as possessions. You realize also that you don't know everything. Most old people think age brought them so much wisdom that they like to give it to young people. I don't feel that way.

I'm close to my grandchildren. They like my company and that is what I'm most happy about. This I'm worried about, that it shouldn't be a duty to take care of me.

I go to Florida once a year for about two or three weeks, and I get myself a hotel way down where the poor people go. There's a nice park where at eight in the morning the old people make exercises. At three, they sing. One comes with a balalaika and it's such a beautiful sight I can't tell you.

ROY VELAZQUEZ *runs a taxi service in Austin, Texas. His office is in the house where he lives with his family and grandchildren. In one room on the ground floor, a young woman sits at a desk with a telephone and radio which she uses to dispatch taxis around town. Outside in the yard, taxis move in and out all day. His sons work with him.*

I was raised with a bunch of people they call Swedes. They was like me. They spoke Swedish, and I spoke Spanish. I couldn't learn too much English from those people. This lady, she call me in the morning when I was a little bitty guy, and she'd say, "Roy, I give you biscuits if you clean up my yard." And that's all we knew. Can't converse. Then I went to school. I went to school three years, and they give the same book. They had no other books in school. When my boys make fun of me, they say, "Daddy, how you gonna stay in business the way you speak?" Well, I'm gonna buy the book and put it in a frame to show all the schooling that I had.

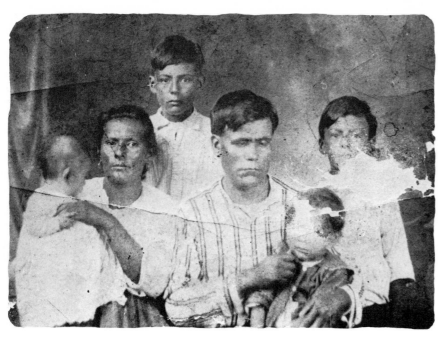

Young Roy Velazquez standing behind his parents

My mother bought me a horse to go to school. She pay six dollars for that horse. It took her six months to pay for it. One day when I was in the school, there came a big snow. When I come out, I see the buzzards flying around and settling on the tree where I tie my horse. MY HORSE! He died, and the buzzards done eat half the horse already. That's when I quit going to school. I tell my kids, "It's not what you learn, it's what you want to do. You can learn a whole lot of things, but if you don't take an interest in what you learn, you ain't never amount to nowhere."

I raised eleven kids. I used to work eighteen hours a day, day in, day out. Anybody can make money. It's a smart man who can save money.

My father comes from Mexico. My father left there because he was working on a farm where he killed a cow. He had to take ten years to pay for it. He escaped to Monterrey where he worked making steel for eight cents a day. Then he met mother. My grandfather did not like him, so he came to the United States, where he worked for four dollars a day. Most people bought from the company store. When the paycheck come in, they take off what you owe the store. Those people, including my father, used to be like slaves. They didn't know about reading. My father die when he was forty-five. He caught pneumonia. He die a very young fellow.

Once I asked my mother to buy me a chicken and a rooster. Soon I had a whole lot of chickens. Then I bought me a cow and then a horse. I used to haul water for the people who worked for the quarry. One day I heard these people talking about a buried treasure under a rock near the school. I knew where the rock was. I took three sticks of dynamite and fifty feet of fuse. By Saturday night I was well organized. I asked my buddy, "Hey, you want to go dig for buried treasure?" He say, "Sure, I'll go with you."

When we got there, we saw the rock and started digging. I had my dynamite in a can of black powder. Black powder don't explode too hard. It just sort of push, but when you put the dynamite in it, it make a big blow. Anyway, we digged until we find the top of a big can. I say, "Don't dig no more, I think here's the money!" We put the dynamite in the side of the rock, so it would push towards the school. We stretch that fifty foot of fuse; we lit and run. We waited a long time, and nothing happened. So we started coming back. We were about a hundred feet away when that thing exploded. That rock went flying through the air, come down, and hit that school right in the middle of the roof. Messed that school all up. Destroyed the school. We run the five miles home through the pastures. Nobody ever knew who blew up the school. Nobody found any treasure either.

I could make a book of the things I've seen.

VACLAV VYTLACIL *is a painter and a teacher.*
His students call him Vyt. He paints in his studio,
which is next to his home in the country. Once a
week he goes into the city to teach and criticize the
work of his students. As a young man he went to
Paris and Italy to paint and there he was influenced
by the modern masters. After seven years he
returned to work and teach. He has been teaching
for over forty years.

I know when I decided to be an artist. I discovered it when I was nine years old, and I've been doing it ever since. I have never wiggled or wobbled. I have never had any other interests except the violin. My parents started me on the violin because my background is Czechoslovak. The Czechs are very musical. Not only very musical but creative. Their crafts are on a very high level. I did both until I discovered I liked being an artist. Drawing, in other words.

I grew up on the West Side of Chicago. One day I was coming home from grammar school when I saw a group of boys about my own age. I was nine then. They all crowded around, trying to see what the one in the middle was showing them. I got interested, so I went over. I had a hard time peeking because they were all excited by what they were seeing. He had a lot of pencil drawings, and he was showing them one after the other. He had the kind of images that we liked. He had a horse and a dog. There was one we all particularly loved. I can still see it today. It was Santa Claus going down the chimney. The snow was indicated with dots all over the paper. We loved the way he did that snow. We just thought this was a miracle. I remember he did one with a very soft black pencil. He shaded that black pencil from a very rich black up to a very light gray. When I caught sight of that, I really thought I could almost eat it. I decided that if he could do that, I could do it too. I began right there.

I didn't start school until I was well over seven. I didn't speak English. I remember when I started school in Kalamazoo, Michigan, nobody was more frightened than I was, as I sat in that seat. I could understand simple English very well, but school! I didn't know what half the words meant. I was too frightened to say anything because I would give it a Czech accent. I could see that I couldn't do what they were doing, so I lived in terror of being humiliated. Finally, the teacher called on me. That was a disaster. I don't remember what happened except I went into semihysterics. The teacher came over and put her arm around me and comforted me. She even took me out in the hall so I could calm myself. That was my first day in school.

When I graduated high school, I couldn't use my geometry or trigonometry or algebra. That to me was a nasty thing that a bunch of nasty old men down at the board of education got together and said, "This is good for the kids." Whenever we got out of the mathematics class, we felt relief.

In my day, a student who had a hard life, was a member of an ethnic group, and whose parents had to work for a living had a certain advantage over those who had it ready-made. He had to join his parents and work as soon as he got old enough. He was prepared for this, and he never forgot it. He had more understanding of the struggle to live.

I have very little feeling about getting old. I

Lecturing to his students

Painting in his studio

carry the same load I always did. I have no troubles of any kind, but I have to say this: I never knew that feet could give out. I thought that if you weren't born with a defect or you didn't cripple yourself afterwards, the feet went on forever. Out of abuse I came to the point where my feet got very tired, and they began to hurt. Well, I said, "So what?" I used to run on the track team, and I got plenty tired enough. But I persisted in standing here in my studio, working on the concrete floor. My feet gave up. I could not walk without pain. I've been doctoring them for about three or four months. I can move around now and forget about them somewhat. When my feet gave out, it brought home the fact I was getting old.

BETTY VYTLACIL *studied painting in Minneapolis, where she met her husband. She went to Europe with her mother and wrote to Mr. Vytlacil, describing her trip. But by the time he finally got to Europe, she had returned home. Then, after many letters from him, she went back to Europe, and they were married there.*

I lived a much more comfortable life as a child than my husband did. I grew up in a very pleasant way without really learning how to be practical. We lived in a nice house. We had servants, and everything was made easy for us. My father used to read aloud to us in the evening. He was very fond of his children. We always had lovely open fires in the evening. We had awfully good food. I had an older sister and a younger brother. We played indoor games like Parcheesi and simple card games. We had dogs and cats.

In winter there was a great deal of snow in Saint Paul. People with horses had sleighs for the winter. In summer the deliveries were all made by wagon. In winter the wagon would be lifted up and put on runners to make it into a sleigh. They went from house to house, delivering things from the shops. What we adored when I was young was called hitching. In the winter we would run out and stand on the runners or hitch our sleds to the back of the delivery sleigh. If the driver was pleasant, you stayed. If not, he would snap his whip and you had to get off. But sometimes you would ride for ages because you never knew how far he was going and you knew he had to go back downtown afterwards. So you would stay on sometimes till after dark. Till he got everything delivered so you could get off and go home. We did it alone, or sometimes two of us did it together. It wasn't dangerous because there were no automobiles. If you fell off, you fell in the snow. Nobody worried about us.

We went to a school called Mrs. Backus's School for Girls. We walked about a mile to school. In the coldest part of the winter, we used to wear Indian moccasins with a lot of socks on our feet.

Recently I had a cataract operation, and my eyes bother me a great deal. I can't read. I was always a great reader. My great grief now is that it never occurred to me that I would come to a point where I was alive and couldn't read. You begin to feel old when physical ailments suddenly attack you. That's what makes you feel old.

HENRY WILSON *lives with his wife, Olla, in Nicodemus, Kansas. This was the original settlement of freed slaves who came from the South to homestead after the Civil War. But today along the main street are the ruins of buildings that housed the businesses of a once thriving community. Mr. Wilson was born in 1878 and Mrs. Wilson in 1893.*

I lived on a farm with my parents. My folks all died. My mother died, my brother died, and my two sisters died. Hard times, you know. I lived off a meal a day when I was a kid. I went two or three winters and never had a pair of shoes. From 1886 on until the present time, winters was like they are now or worse. I've had a hard time all my life. I've worked for twenty-seven cents a day. I tell a lot of people about the way I lived. They look kinda funny. I think that they think I lied. I just grew up with no education. All the education I ever got was three months. When I was sixteen years old, I couldn't write my name. From then on I had enough ambition to keep trying to get so I could write and read. And I did. I can read.

Mrs. Wilson holds a picture of an early home.

We used to live in sod houses. To make a sod house, you take a team and plow the sod on the prairie. The sod will lay over on the ground. The grass holds it together. Then you take a spade and cut it into pieces. Then you lay it up for walls, just like you do brick. For the roof we put pole rafters up on top. Then you take cane or stalks of sunflower sticks and lay it on. Then you put dirt on top the cane. You use a certain kind of dirt; it's a magnesia stone all crushed. The magnesia is like clay, but it would melt better and cover the cracks so the roof doesn't leak.

I've slept many a time with three of four places leaking in the house. You'd have old tubs and buckets to catch the water. Sod houses and dugouts, they leaked a lot of times . . . and a lot of times they didn't. A sod house is cool in the summer and warm in the winter. I'd never known one to burn in a prairie fire. I could build a sod house now if I could work and had the sod. But the sod's got too rotten. You can't use it no more.

I've seen them have a big sod house and have dances on them dirt floors. Dust would smother you. You had to take a bucket of water and sprinkle the floors, let it settle the dust, you know, then go back to dancing. There was always somebody who could play an old guitar or play an old fiddle and make some kind of music. Square dances, that's what they had. Waltzing and all this late stuff, why, we never saw none of it. People didn't do that kind of dancing. They'd square dance on that old dirt floor, and that dirt would get gray. The first schoolhouse near where I lived was a little bitty sod schoolhouse. My sister went to school in that old sod schoolhouse.

My wife's father had a picnic ground. We used to have great picnics. There'd be sometimes a thousand people on that ground, white and colored. People associated together. Oh yes. People had hard times and good times. Everybody was friendly then.

LULU MAE CRAIG *was one of the first settlers of Nicodemus, Kansas, where she grew up, taught school, and married. Later she and her family moved to Colorado. She lived on her homestead in La Junta, Colorado, with two of her daughters until she passed away at the age of one hundred and two. These anecdotes were recorded shortly after she celebrated her hundredth birthday.*

Neighbors offering birthday greetings

My father could read and write. He belonged to a master who had some children. When the children came home from school, they would sit around a table and study their lessons. My dad would point, and they'd spell. They always studied the alphabet, and my dad'd remember. That is how many slaves learned to read.

When freedom came to the states, a good many of the slaves stayed where they were. The master would say, "Stay and I'll give you something." But some other masters kick them off the place. They didn't have any money and nowhere to go. It was an unhandy place to live.

I remember the day we left for Nicodemus. I was less than six years old. We traveled by wagon. It took us about four weeks to go about three hundred fifty miles.

When we arrived, we couldn't see Nicodemus anywhere. We knowed we got there, yet we couldn't see it. We unhitched the team and asked a man what hill it was kept us from seeing Nicodemus. He just laughed and laughed. The reason we couldn't see it was because everyone lived in a dugout. There wasn't a house on top of the ground.

A dugout is like a cellar. It has a dirt roof and is made of the sod plowed from the prairie. When we arrived in 1879, there were as many as two or three hundred people living in the dugouts. Each day they would leave their dugouts to homestead their land.

When the first settlers arrived in Nicodemus, there were Indians there. They must have been Comanche or Cheyenne. They had a place in the northwest country, where the government gave supplies to the Indians. The homesteaders were always talking about the Indians doing so many bad things. They were afraid they'd come.

One day someone said they saw Indians riding. The settlers ran and hid in some grottoes down beside the riverbank. The Indians knew where they were. One Indian called out, "Ho, dark face, come out. You needn't be scared. Indian no hurt you." When they were all out, he

Mrs. Craig (the teacher) with her class in Nicodemus

asked, "What do you have to eat?" "Nothing," they said. The Indians all laughed. There must have been as many as a hundred ponies. The chief waved his hand, and they got their horses in a circle. He threw out a bag of food; it was beans. Every one of them fellows threw out something—beans, sugar, coffee, meat, bags of meal. After that the Indians rode away. Didn't say anything, just waved their hands. Indians didn't talk very much. They had been to the fort and gotten their allowances, which they divided with the settlers. The Indians never molested them in any way.

Some sod houses didn't have any floor at all. They'd just sweep the earth and smooth it down. I know one woman hated this floor because she couldn't scrub it. She poured on water, and it was muddy for two days. That was the way people found out how to get rid of fleas.

Fleas lived in the dust of the floors. If you didn't bother to wet the floor, the fleas would get up on the bed at night. Oh, they were a terrible pest, biting people. At night you could stand on a chair and get undressed and put a nightgown on. Then hop over into bed. That way the fleas wouldn't crawl up your feet.

We played lots of games. At picnics we played crack the whip, we pitched horseshoes, and we played hopscotch. At parties we'd play two in the ring, catch her and kiss her, and old witch. King William was a game where we sang:

> King William was King James' son
> Upon the royal throne he run.
> Upon his breast he wore a star
> And in his mouth a big cigar.
> So choose you east or choose you west
> Choose the one you love the best.

I never cease to miss the friends we had in Nicodemus. I go over the trails of the past often, very often. I miss them even when they are far away, when I hear that they are gone forever. It's a saddening thing to think that I will not see any of those people anymore. They were so much a part of my life, the parties, the dances. Some of the fellows were such excellent dancers. Those are the things you miss, the things that live in your memory.

Acknowledgements

*I would like to thank the people who helped
me make this book: the friends and strangers
who introduced me to the people I interviewed;
Trini McClintock and Susan Gurnee, who
transcribed the long hours of tape recordings;
Dr. Harry Ploski, who enabled me to go to
Colorado and Nicodemus; Beth Cummins, who
helped me make the prints for the book; Ann
Troy and Riki Levinson, for their patience,
encouragement, and gentle criticism.*

*And especially those who let me visit with
them to talk and photograph them. Those who
were included in the book and those who were
not have all become a rich part of my life.*

                    Thank you.